This book belongs to
....

Katha Chitrakala Award

Katha Chitrakala Awards recognize exemplary children's book illustrations and concepts. Artists with that magical eye and a way with colours are invited to this international search for excellence – the only one of its kind in India – open to all image storytellers, emerging or established, to make an indelible mark in the world of children's books.

Today, Katha Chitrakala Awards boasts of an enthusiastic participation of over 300 illustrators from over 14 countries.

Katha has a real soft corner for kids. Which is why it ... create[s] such gorgeous picture books for children.   — Time Out

About Katha

Katha, a nonprofit organization working with and in story and storytelling since 1988, is one of India's top publishing houses. Katha's main focus is on introducing an array of writings from the many oral and written traditions of India to children, ages 0-17. Classy productions, child-friendly layouts and superb illustrations go in tandem with excellent writing. Katha works with 6,000 Friends of Katha and a growing pool of writers, translators and literary enthusiasts. Our constant striving is for greater reach and impact amongst teachers and students, policy makers and the corporate sector.

Our mission: To enhance the joys of reading. To help every child realize his/her potential through community enriching, quality learning so that no child lives in poverty. To help break down gender, social, cultural and economic stereotypes through story and storytelling. And to enhance the role of translation as a counter-divisive tool in nation building.

Our belief: Stories help create friendships of a rare kind to culturelink people, faiths and creative impulses. Stories are the life-savers of future nations.

Our credo: Uncommon creativities for a common good.

She skims like a bird on the foam of a stream,

She floats like a laugh
from the lips of a dream.

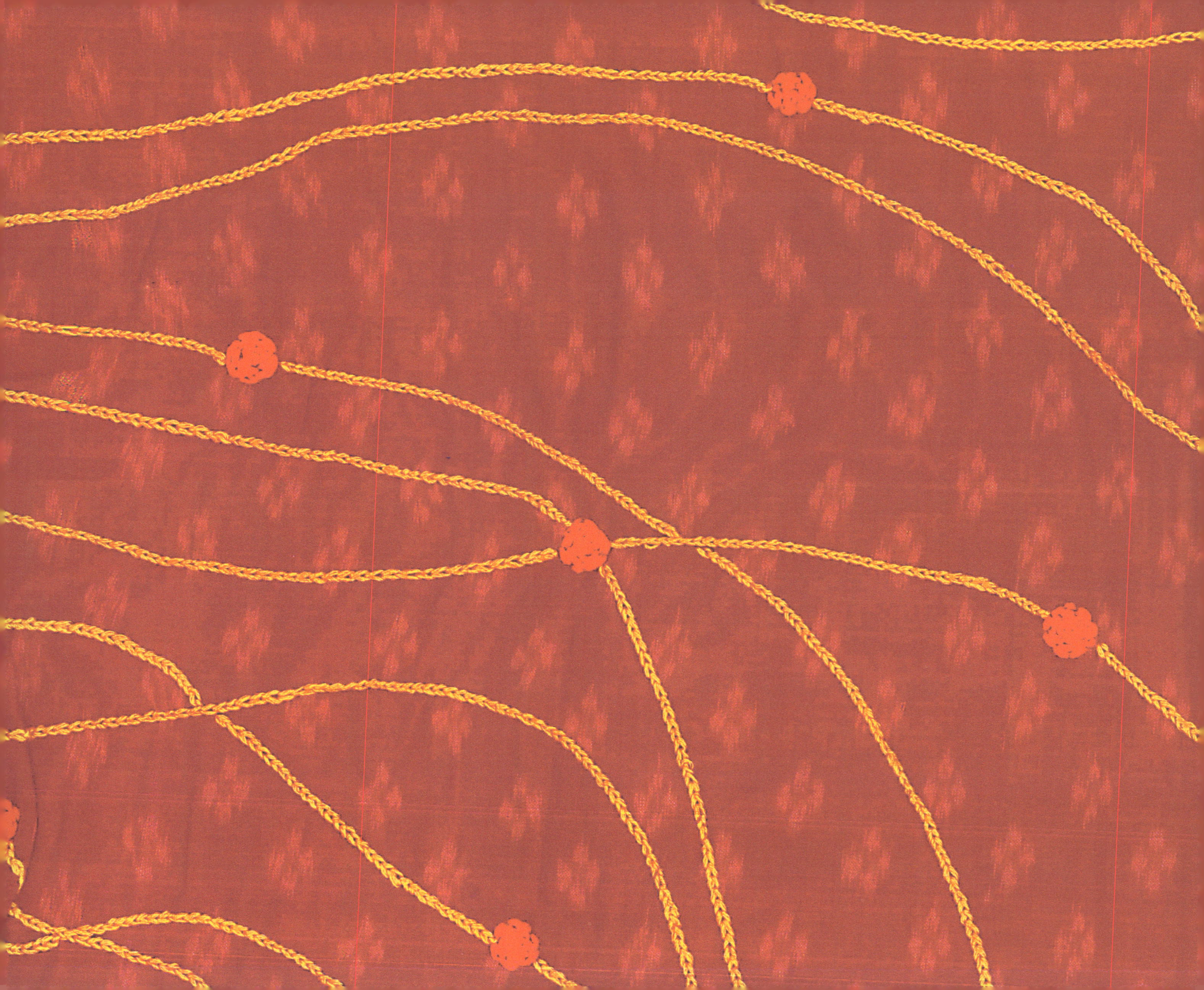

We bear her along
like a pearl on a string.

Softly, O softly
we bear her along,

She hangs like a star
in the dew of our song;

She springs like a beam
on the brow of the tide,

She falls like a tear
from the eyes of a bride.

Lightly, O lightly
we glide and we sing,

We bear her along
like a pearl on a string.

SAROJINI NAIDU
(1879 - 1949)

Sarojini Naidu was the eldest child of Bengali poetess Sundari Devi and the scientist, philosopher and linguist Aghornath Chattopadhyaya. Just like her mother, Sarojini had a love of words from a young age. Recognizing her talent, the Nizam of Hyderabad sent her to study at the King's College, London at the age of sixteen.

Her first major collection of poems, '*The Golden Threshold*' was published in 1905. Two other collections, '*The Bird of Time*' (1912) and '*The Broken Wing*' (1917) were also published to great acclaim. Known for the lyrical qualities of her poems, she earned the sobriquet 'Nightingale of India.'

Closely involved in the movement for Indian Independence, she travelled across the country, spreading the message of freedom and nationalism through her rousing speeches. Her dedication to the cause of Independence led to her becoming the first woman Governor of Uttar Pradesh and the second woman President of the Indian National Congress.

MEET OTHER WONDROUS WOMEN WRITERS

AMRITA PRITAM was born in Gujranwala in present-day Pakistan and is one of India's best loved writers from Punjab. Settling in Delhi, she wrote in her mother tongue Punjabi and in Hindi too.

Her writings were influenced by famous Punjabi epics such as *Heer Ranja* as well as contemporary events such as the Jallianwala Massacre of 1919. A prolific writer, Amrita penned 28 novels and various volumes of prose, short stories and poems. She became the first woman to win the Sahitya Akademi Award in 1956. Later she also received the Padma Shri Award (1969), the Bhartiya Jnanpith Award (1982) and the Padma Vibhushan Award (2004).

INDIRA GOSWAMI, renowned Assamese poet, writer and scholar was popularly called Mamoni Baideo. Her first short stories were published when she was just thirteen years old.

Her most famous works are inspired by harsh realities she experienced, such as widowhood (*Neel Kanthi Braja*), social issues and political happenings (*Tej Aru Dhulire Dhushorito Prishtha*). She received the Sahitya Akademi Award (1983) and India's highest literary award, the Jnanpith Award (2001).

KAMALA SURAIYYA, one of Kerala's best known writers, is widely known by her pen name Madhavi Kutty. Born to a poetess mother and journalist father, Kamala started writing and publishing in both English and Malayam by the age of fifteen.

Her brutally honest writings dealt with human emotions and relationships, often questioning the existing codes of society. Her most famous Malayali work is the autobiographical '*Ente Katha*' which has been translated into 15 languages. Among her famous English works are '*The Soul Knows How to Sing*' and '*Summer in Calcutta*'. Kamala received many honours including a Nobel Prize Nomination (1984), Asian Poetry Prize (1998) and Sahitya Academy Award (2003).

Indu Harikumar has studied both fashion and history. She stumbled into the world of picture books by chance. A Mumbai-based prolific blogger, she has written and illustrated for various publishing houses - NGOs, government bodies and MNCs. She enjoys upcycling trash and calls herself a fabric fiend.

KATHA

First published © Katha 2012
Copyright © Katha, 2012
Text copyright © Katha, 2012
Illustrations copyright © Indu Harikumar, 2012
All rights reserved. No part of this book may be reproduced or utilized in any form without the prior written permission of the publisher.
Fax: 2651 4373
E-mail: marketing@katha.org, Website: www.katha.org

KATHA is a registered nonprofit devoted to enhancing the joys of reading amongst children and adults. Katha Schools are situated in the slums and streets of Delhi and tribal villages of Arunachal Pradesh.
A3 Sarvodaya Enclave, Sri Aurobindo Marg
New Delhi 110 017
Phone: 4141 6600, 4182 9998, 2652 1752

Ten per cent of sales proceeds from this book will support the quality education of children studying in Katha Schools.
Katha regularly plants trees to replace the wood used in the making of its books.

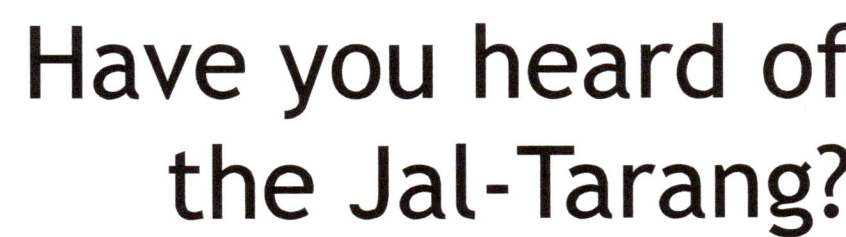

Have you heard of the Jal-Tarang?

It is an Indian melodic percussion instrument which is made up of a set of bowls filled with water at different levels. When you strike the edges of the bowls with a beater (wooden stick) you will hear gentle tinkle sounds.

Earlier bronze or porcelain cups were used, but now artists usually use china bowls. Water is poured into 16 bowls and the pitch is changed by adjusting the volume of water in the bowls. Larger bowls produce lower octaves while smaller ones produce higher octaves. As many as 22 bowls can be used in a Jal-Tarang and the players arrange them in a semi circle formation in front of them.

Jal-Tarang literally means "waves in water" but indicates motion of sound created or modified with the aid of water.

You can make your own Jal-Tarang too!

Take 6- 9 bowls (metal, ceramic or china) and fill them with water at different levels, starting with an empty bowl and ending with a full bowl.

Now strike the bowls lightly at the edges with a metal spoon or a wooden stick and hear them tinkle! Make your own tunes and remember to keep practicing.

www.ingramcontent.com/pod-product-compliance
Lightning Source LLC
Chambersburg PA
CBHW040027100426
42743CB00005BA/134